Finance

Getting Your Books Up and Running

A Handy Reference Guide for Entrepreneurs

Debbie Richard

Butterflies Pause Inc.

© 2022 Butterflies Pause Inc.
ISBN 979-8-9855064-1-9

Publisher: Butterflies Pause Inc.
                Grand Junction, Colorado 81507

Contents

Reader Alert

This book is intended to be a reference guide for a small or new business owner regarding how to select an accounting system, get a good set of books up and running, interface with external finance/ operating systems, and avoid some common accounting pitfalls. It is not intended to be a comprehensive manual addressing all finance keeping issues, but is rather a conveniently organized source of basic system information that can be used to assess, implement, and manage a financial operating system. Importantly, information contained in this guide may be outdated or inaccurate as technology is ever changing.

Don't wait until your financial records become a great big mess to learn about how to set-up and manage your books...

Introduction

I've been a volunteer business coach for start-up and development companies since I retired almost six years ago. During this time, I have met with clients in every stage of the business life cycle, and the amazing thing is, almost all of them have struggled with keeping a good set of books. Most have already started a business, often using a spreadsheet to keep track of their finances. Some have been using a software program rather haphazardly, and some have actually hired a bookkeeper to get the job done. Whatever the case may be, by the time the client comes to see me, their financial records are often a mess, a jarring term I know, but...

BEWARE! *A casual state of disarray in your records can quickly become a great big mess!*

The good news is, you can avoid this kind of catastrophe by getting a good set of books up and running right from the start. And the even better news is, you can do this all by yourself if you are willing to spend some quality time learning a bit about bookkeeping systems and financial accounting. You won't be an expert, but you should have the basic knowledge required to manage your own set of books, read some financial statements, and talk with bankers. This reference guide is designed to help you do this.

In Part 1, we explore selecting the right finance system. We look at the various QuickBooks (QB) plans available. In Part 2, we learn how to set-up a Chart of Accounts, the foundation of any accounting system. In Part 3, we explore QB interfaces with external systems you might want to use, and then in Part 4, we talk about possible pitfalls when a non-accountant creates a set of books and does the ongoing record keeping. In summary, with the help of this reference guide and some personal diligence, by the time you are ready to start making money, you should have a stable financial accounting system ready to manage your finances.

So—let's get started!

Why QuickBooks is the popular choice:

Scalability—A business can grow with this system.

Training Resources—They are abundant and many are free.

Data Sharing—Most tax professionals use these programs.

Versatility—Plans integrate with many third party applications.

Part 1- Selecting the Right Finance System

Quick Books is a financial recordkeeping system that allows you to process automated financial transactions using an accounting framework called the Chart of Accounts. It can be purchased either as an online program or as a desktop program. Online programs are cloud based. They allow you to access your records anytime you have an internet connection and a web based device. Desktop programs reside on your local computer. You download the software to use it. Both Programs work for most small and medium sized companies and while there are many other finance system alternatives, QB is by far the most popular choice.

One, QB is scalable. You can easily grow with this software. Two, there are abundant training resources available and many of them are free. Three, most accounting and tax professionals use this program, so you will be able to share your data with them. And four, it offers versatility as it integrates with over 700 third party applications. Moreover, there are two programs and seven different plans available with various levels of functionality which scale with price. We will explore the differences between the two programs and then the plans by doing a high level Program comparison followed by a Plan comparison within each Program.

But before we get started, let's define the term Finance Keeping, a term I dubbed myself, and consider your business needs in terms of Finance Keeping requirements.

The Term "Finance Keeping"

I started to use the term "Finance Keeping" to broadly describe all of the aspects of daily financial recordkeeping. I did this because the world in general seems to be confused regarding what I consider to be the three basic elements of any financial system used to keep a good set of books: 1) comprehensive bookkeeping functions, 2) accounting aptness, and 3) robust reports for financial analysis. Most folks refer to these elements collectively as "Bookkeeping". Some use the term "Accounting", and some might even mention "Financial Analysis", but most of them don't seem to realize that *ALL* of these elements are required if a business owner wants to properly manage the company's finances.

So—there you have it! The concept of Finance Keeping is born!

Ok, maybe you think I'm being a bit academic, but when it's time for you to purchase a system or hire somebody to manage all or some of your finances, I want you to get the most for your money. And that's why I want to explore each of these elements with you and then come back to this thing I call "Finance Keeping".

1) Bookkeeping and Bookkeeping Functions—

Bookkeeping refers to a basic number tracking process that allows a user to input and classify cash coming into the company and cash going out by tagging these items as sales, purchases, equipment, rent and various other labels, which puts them into buckets called accounts. A Comprehensive Bookkeeping system will include payroll processing, inventory tracking, customer invoicing and collections, and purchase order processing.

Basically, a Bookkeeping system helps keep the business owner from going broke and possibly filing for bankruptcy.

2) Accounting and Accounting Aptness—

In simple terms, Accounting refers to a Comprehensive Bookkeeping process that complies with rules and guidelines established by regulatory bodies. A business owner is able to generate information needed for sales and payroll tax forms, annual income tax returns, and financial statements required by investors, bankers, auditors, and tax accountants.

Basically, an Accounting system helps keep the business owner from breaking government rules and going to jail. Ok, I'm kidding...kind of.

3) Financial Analysis and Robust Reporting—

Financial Analysis refers to a diagnostic process whereby a user is able to download data from an Accounting system and use the data to review and interpret trends, prepare performance reports, budgets, forecasts, cashflow scenarios, and various other types of management reports. Some Accounting systems allow a business owner to analyze operating trends in a production department, at a branch office, by product or service delivered, by profit or cost center, and many other important categories.

Basically, a state-of-the art Accounting system like this helps a business owner grow and make money.

In summary, Finance Keeping includes the process of managing cashflow via a bookkeeping system, compliance with government rules and regulations via a system with accounting aptness, and financial analysis via a system with robust reporting. Bottom line—good Finance Keeping helps the business owner grow and make money. So, as we move forward, keep this definition in mind when completing the Systems Requirements Checklist coming up next, and selecting a QB Program and Plan.

Your Finance Keeping system should help you with:

- Cash—Managing cash so you don't go broke,

- Compliance—Following rules so you don't go to jail, and

- Analysis—Interpreting trends so you grow and make money.

Finance Keeping Requirements

Let's take a few moments now and consider your Finance Keeping requirements for the next two to three years. The Checklist on the next page is a list of functional requirements, which can be tailored and used to assess your business needs and make a decision regarding which of the QuickBooks Plans best meets your needs. The columns are described below.

Column 1—Functional Requirements

The first column presents a core list of functional requirements. You can tailor these needs by adding and/or subtracting requirements.

Column 2—Y/N

The next column called "Y/N" is a priority column. "Y" or "Yes" indicates your business requires this software function. "N" or "No" indicates the function is not needed. You can also add a "P" for preferred, but not necessary, or any other code you might desire.

Column 3—O/D

The third column labelled "O/D" indicates which QB Program offers this feature. "O" indicates "Online" and "D" indicates "Desktop". "O/D" indicates that the feature is offered in both QB programs or you can use "B" for both.

Column 4—Plan

The fourth column called "Plan" indicates which Plan is required for this function to be operable. Select the Plan from the Online and Desktop comparison charts.

Column 5—Ref

The last column called "Ref" for Reference is a place to keep track of comments/questions. A number in this column indicates there is a numbered note following the table. You can add more columns as desired to track other relevant information such as price or number of users required.

System Requirements Checklist

Functional Requirements	Y/N	O/D	Plan	Ref
Bank account and credit card reconciliations				
Bill payment and vendor management				
Purchase Order Tracking				
Customer invoicing and receivable tracking				
Mileage tracking				
Time reporting for staff				
Inventory management				
Project profitability				
Class tracking (departments, locations, other)				
Large number of users				
QuickBooks access away from the office				
Specialized industry needs				
Ability to track multiple companies				
Sales tax reporting				
Payroll processing				
Estimates and order tracking				
Sales order fulfillment				
Mobile receipt capture				
Employee expense reimbursements				
Batch processing				
Forecasting				
Large volume of data and list categories				

Use your Systems Requirements Checklist to select a Program and then a Plan—first a Program and then a Plan. And remember...

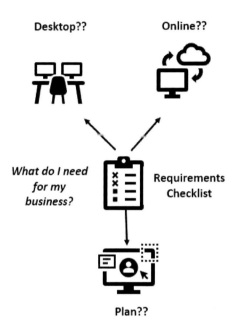

- *Pricing scales with the number and type of features,*
- *Features differ from Program to Program and Plan to Plan,*
- *The fee for the Online Program is monthly,*
- *The fee for the Desktop Program is lump sum once a year, and*
- *You can transition from Program to Program and Plan to Plan.*

Selecting a QuickBooks Program and Plan

Ok...now you are ready to take a good look at the QB Programs and Plans. We will start by comparing the Online Program to the Desktop Program. We will look at pricing, number of users, transactions, number of companies, and some high level features. Based on this information, you may be able to select a QB Program immediately using your System Requirements Checklist. If not, you will have a pretty good idea about what is available online vs. on your local desktop. Then we will look at the plans within each Program and consider what features may be important to you within each Plan.

The first thing you will probably see is that pricing scales with the number and type of available features. Like almost everything else in this world, the more you pay, the more you get. The next thing you will probably see is that features differ from Program to Program and Plan to Plan. That's why I want you to look at the Program first and then the Plan. And the next thing you will probably notice is that you pay for the QB Online Program on a monthly basis while you pay for the QB Desktop Program lump sum once a year. Yes, there are lots of things to consider, but— there is no need to fret.

Use your Checklist to select a Program and Plan that best meets your needs for at least the next two years and know this—you can transition from Program to Program and Plan to Plan. It's not something you want to do frequently, especially if you decide to change Programs as the dashboard and processes are very different even though the features may be the same. This is also true when you upgrade a Plan, although the differences between Plans are not as dramatic as the dashboard is pretty consistent among the Plans within a Program.

Now—let's take a look at the two different Programs.

Program Comparison Chart—Online vs. Desktop[1]

Before choosing a Program, carefully review your Systems Requirements Checklist which presents your business needs for the next 2 years, read the notes regarding Functional Differences, and keep in mind that you can move between programs if your needs change.

Plan Features		Online Program			Desktop Program		
Note			*Monthly*	*Annual*			*Annual*
(1)	**Pricing:**	Simple Start	$ 25	$ 300	Pro		$ 350
		Essentials	$ 50	$ 600	Premier		$ 550
		Plus	$ 80	$ 960	Enterprise		$ 1,275
		Advanced	$ 180	$ 2,160			
(2)	**User Max:**	Simple Start	1		Pro		3
		Essentials	3		Premier		5
		Plus	5		Enterprise		40
		Advanced	25				
		Base Price	All		*Base Price*		1
	Unlimited Transactions		X				---
(3)	Unlimited Companies		---				X
	Project Accounting		X				X
	Inventory Management		X				X
	Fixed Asset Accounting		---				---
	Free Upgrade		X				X
	Unlimited Customer Support		X				X
	30-day Free Trial		X				---
	60-day Money-back Guarantee		---				X
	Automatic Off-site Backup		X				X
(4)	Mobile Receipt Capture		X				X
(5)	Access Anywhere-Any Device		X				---
(6)	Industry-specific Editions		---				X
(7)	Tax Pro Access		X				X
(8)	Bookkeeping Assistance		X				X

---

[1] Information contained in this table may be outdated as technology updates and pricing are dynamic.

Notes Regarding Functional Differences

1. **Pricing**—The Online program is a monthly subscription with a limited number of concurrent users. The Desktop program is available as an annual subscription with additional benefits.

2. **Simultaneous Users**—QB Online comes with a set number of users included in the subscription price. All users can access the program simultaneously. QB Desktop can also handle multiple users, but only one user at a time can access the program unless an additional fee is paid.

3. **Mobile App**—QB Online has a mobile app capable of performing most of the functions needed to keep a set of books. The app available for the Desktop Program can only be used for capturing cash receipts.

4. **Multiple Companies**—QB Desktop allows you to manage more than one company.

5. **Cloud vs. Desktop**—The main difference between QuickBooks Online and QuickBooks Desktop is that QuickBooks Online is a cloud-based accounting program, and QuickBooks Desktop is locally-installed.

6. **Industry Specific Software**—The online version of QB does not have industry-specific editions. Desktop has editions available for seven different industries.

7. **Sharing with Your Tax Pro**—Both Online and Desktop programs allow you to give your external accountant access to your books without impacting the number of users allowed to work in the program. The Desktop version, however, requires you to make a copy of your data and transfer it to your accountant. Any changes made by your accountant must be imported into your company file.

8. **Bookkeeping Assistance**—Both programs have assistance for keeping your books. With the Online Program, you can consult with an Online Pro Advisor as part of the basic fee. For the Desktop Program, your only option is an independent QuickBooks ProAdvisor who may charge you for consulting services. That said, there is a tremendous amount of free help available on the internet for features in both QB Programs.

QuickBooks Online Plans

Important Considerations

Online plans are cloud based and as a result, they may be the best choice for companies whose staff need access to the QB program anywhere and at any time. They also have the added benefit of giving your accountant real time access to your financial records and integrate nicely with many e-commerce platforms. Unlike the Desktop plans, sales tax is automatically calculated when an invoice is processed based on the customer's address, and there are no additional fees for extra users to have concurrent access. That said, there is a limit on the number of users for each plan ranging from 1 to a maximum of 25.

One other thing to consider is data backup. Even though the Online Plans backup your data automatically, this data is only kept for a year and may not be immediately available in the event of a crash. As a safeguard, you can purchase the Advanced Plan. But beware— even if you purchase this Plan with a backup solution, you are not able to back up all of your data. There is a very long list of data excluded. Be sure to refer to this list before selecting a Plan.

Summary of Benefits:

- Access to QB anywhere at anytime for users in all plans,

- Real time access for outside accountants,

- Sales tax automatically calculated on invoices,

- No add-on fees for extra users, although the maximum number is 25.

Online Plans Comparison Chart[1]

Plan Features		Simple Start	Essentials	Plus	Advanced
Cost:	*Monthly*	$12.50	$25.00	$40.00	$90.00
	Annual	$ 150.00	$ 300.00	$ 480.00	$ 1,080.00
Multiple Users		*1*	*Up to 3*	*Up to 5*	*Up to 25*
Income and expenses		X	X	X	X
Invoice and payments		X	X	X	X
Tax deductions		X	X	X	X
Powerful reports		X	X	X	X
Receipt capture		X	X	X	X
Mileage tracking		X	X	X	X
Cash flow		X	X	X	X
Sales and sales tax		X	X	X	X
Estimates		X	X	X	X
Contractors		X	X	X	X
Bill management			X	X	X
Enter time			X	X	X
Inventory				X	X
Project profitability				X	X
Class Tracking				X	X
Business analytics with Excel					X
Employee expenses					X
Batch invoices and expenses					X
Customized access					X
Exclusive Premium Apps					X
Dedicated account team					X
On-demand training					X
Workflow automation					X
Data restoration					X

1 Information contained in this table may be outdated as technology updates and pricing are dynamic.

QuickBooks Desktop Plans

Important Considerations

Desktop plans are optimal for companies that need to manage multiple businesses, operate in specialized industries, want to process a payroll locally, monitor sales orders through a fulfillment process, manage a large amount of data, have a large number of concurrent users, and want to maintain backups of their data for an unlimited period of time. There are seven specialized industries available: construction and contractors, retail, professional services, manufacturing, wholesale and distribution, accountants, and nonprofit companies. End to end sales order fulfillment offers a better and easier workflow for sales orders using a fulfillment worksheet, a mobile scanner, and automated shipping labels. Large List Limits allow companies to process large amounts of data in a large number of categories, and the maximum concurrent user capacity is 40.

Incidentally—the Enterprise version of the Desktop Program can be used in the cloud if this add-on feature is purchased.

Summary of Benefits:

• Able to manage multiple companies,

• Processing systems tailored for specialized industries,

• Able to accommodate a large number of simultaneous users,

• End to end sales order fulfillment,

• Large List Limits,

• Able to store data backups off site for an unlimited period of time.

Desktop Plans Comparison Chart[1]

Plan Features	Pro	Premier	Enterprise
Cost[a]:	$ 349.99	$ 549.99	$ 1,206.00
	Subscription	Subscription	Subscription
Concurrent Users	Up to 3	Up to 5	Up to 40
Track income & expenses	X	X	X
Invoicing	X	X	X
Run Reports	100+	150+	200+
	Basic	Industry	Advanced
Track sales tax	X	X	X
Send estimates	X	X	X
Track sales & sales tax	X	X	X
Manage bills & Accounts payable	X	X	X
Enter time	X	X	X
Track inventory	X	X	X
List limits	X	X	X
Pay 1099 contractors	X	X	X
Unlimited support	X	X	VIP
Data backups and upgrades	X	X	X
Class Tracking	X	X	X
Job (Project) Tracking	X	X	X
Forecasting		X	X
Industry specific features		X	X
Mobile inventory barcode scanning	----	----	X
End to end sales order fulfillment	----	----	X
Payroll	Add-on	Add-on	Add-on
Cloud access	----	----	Add-on

[a] Cost does not include Add-on features

---

1 Information contained in this table may be outdated as technology updates are continuous.

21

Learning Topics:

Step 1—Understand how a Chart of Accounts is structured.

Step 2—Understand how accounts are used to process transactions.

Step 3—Understand how accounts produce financial reports.

Part 2- Setting Up a Chart of Accounts

The Chart of Accounts (COA) is a list of accounts used to categorize financial transactions and produce accurate and meaningful reports to help effectively manage your business. It is the heart of any financial reporting system, and if used properly, you will be able to manage your cash, your inventory, your customer and vendor accounts, and generate reports containing valuable information regarding the health and profitability of your business. You will also have the information you need to efficiently file federal and state tax returns, sales tax returns, and prepare comprehensive cashflow projections.

The good news is you don't have to be a financial expert to set up and use the QB system. It's fairly user friendly once you learn the basics, and the even better news is that if you get stuck, you can hop on the internet to get some help, or take a class to expedite your learning curve.

The first step is to understand how a COA is structured and what part QB plays related to getting it started. The next step is to learn about how the various types of accounts in the COA are used to drive transactional processes, and the last step is to learn about how the accounts produce financial reports.

Step 1—Understanding the Structure

QB automatically sets up a basic COA for you. In some of the Desktop plans, QB asks you to select an industry and once you make this selection, QB automatically adds industry specific accounts to help you get started. And now, with this foundation, you can customize your COA as you see fit by adding or subtracting Parent and Sub Accounts and Account Descriptions. You can also turn on an account number feature, manage your tax information using a feature called "Tax Line Item Mapping", manage data security, and track your company results by class and by job—hidden features in QB that work with the COA.

Parent and Sub Accounts and Account Descriptions

When the basic COA is loaded into your company, you will see a long list of what I like to call Parent Accounts, an account capable of containing lower-level accounts underneath it. Each of these accounts has an Account Type, a Tax Line Item, and an Account Description. You can add more Parent Accounts to the chart if you like, and/or you can add Sub Accounts underneath the Parent Accounts to track further details about the Parent Account. You will also see a place to put an account description to further assist you in understanding what type of transactions are in the account. Importantly, these Accounts and Account Descriptions appear in numerous output reports.

The Parent Accounts and the Sub Accounts will appear in the primary financial reports presented to outside professionals like bankers and investors. The account descriptions will appear in transactional reports often used by management. Thus, proper spelling, word capitalization, and professional account names is highly recommended. And—one other thing you should know before you start adding and changing accounts, QB adds words automatically to your Account names, words already associated with the Account.

Let's say you want to track Auto Expense and some underlying details about this expense. The first thing you do is set up a Parent Account called "Auto". You don't need to add the word "Expense" because QB will pick up that word from the Account Type you select: Expense. Next, you will set up the Sub Accounts: Insurance, Fuel, and Maintenance.

You don't need to add the word Auto because QB will pick up this word on its own from the Parent Account name. You can then add a description to these accounts to help you remember what kinds of transactions you want to track, and when you're done, the COA will look something like the table inside of the dashed line box you see below, depending upon which QB program you are using. The Sub Accounts may be indented under the Parent Account as you see below, or the Parent Account may appear in the COA four times. Auto will appear by itself, and then Auto will appear three more times with a colon followed by the Sub Account name.

Added for clarification	Account	Type	Account Description
Parent	Auto	Expense	Maintenance vehicles
Sub Account	Insurance	Expense	General Coverage
Sub Account	Fuel	Expense	Gas and Oil
Sub Account	Maintenance	Expense	Repairs and Parts

Bottom line—you are only entering the words under the headings Account and Account Description. And by the way, what you see on the screen may not be the same as what you see if you print a COA report, which you don't really need to do.

Account Number Feature

Account numbers are important because they help ensure accounts are properly categorized by Account Type as numbers are assigned by Type. They also help you arrange reports into meaningful sections, groups, or categories. That said, most small companies do not use this feature because there is usually only one user maintaining accounts, so the risk of error when it comes to selecting an Account Type is lower. Larger companies with multiple users accessing accounts almost always use account numbers.

Tax Line Item Mapping

Tax Line Items are used to map transactions into Tax Forms in preparation for filing tax returns. Most small companies do not use this feature as it requires a fair amount of tax knowledge. They rely upon their tax accountant to extract numbers from QB data and file returns.

Larger companies or companies who have a staff member with some tax experience may opt to use this feature. Thus, you only need to fill in the Tax Line Item category if you are planning to use QB information to generate tax forms.

Security

Once you complete your COA, don't forget to consider the issue of security. The various QB programs have password security access that allows you to set up multiple users with levels of restricted access. This practice will minimize errors and possible fraud. For instance, let's say you want your office manager to be able to invoice customers, but you don't want to give this person access to your bank accounts or payroll processing. You can set-up a password for this staff member with access restricted to customer accounts.

This kind of protection is important, so please take a moment to find and explore this feature before allowing users to access your accounts.

Hidden Features-Class and Job (Project)

There are two features in QB that work with the COA that need to be in your frame of reference before you begin setting up your accounts: Class and Job or Project, depending upon which QB program you're using. These features will help minimize the number of accounts you might need to set up as they allow you to track information by classification such as department, location, or cost center, and to track information by job or project within these classifications. For now, make a note that these features do not appear in the COA table and—are not available in all QB plans. We will talk more about these features shortly.

Step 2—Understanding Accounts

Accounts are the heart and soul of any good accounting system, and that's why understanding the basics of how a COA works is important. We will examine three aspects of Accounts: Account types, which drive financial reporting, Utility Accounts, which are at the core of processing transactions efficiently, and the use of Class and Job/Project identifiers, which simplify segment reporting. Collectively, these features along with Accounts allow a business owner to organize and manage a company successfully.

Account Types and Detail Types

Every account must have an Account Type. The Account Type designates where transactions will appear in financial reports. In some QB plans, you must also set-up a Detail Type. These Detail Types do not impact the accounting in your books. They are only there to help you choose the right Account Type. QB will first ask you for an Account Type, and based on this type it will present the Detail Type options you have. You cannot edit, add, or delete types. You must choose the ones closest to what you need.

You can, however, eliminate Accounts you don't want to use. This practice ensures transactions are not erroneously posted to these accounts by users. It also cleans up report formats. Unfortunately, once an account has been used, it cannot be deleted, even if it has a zero balance. Instead, you must mark this account as "Inactive" by clicking on "Action" or "Account" inside the COA .

Utility Accounts

Certain types of accounts have automated functionality features. These accounts should only be used when you understand how the automated features work. Generally, you should not make what is called a Journal Entry, a manual method for recording a business transaction, in any of these accounts as these manual entries are likely to create reconciliation problems and cause accounts to be inaccurate. The Utility Accounts are presented below.

Accounts	Automated Functionality
Bank	Bank download and reconciliation processes
Accounts Receivable	Invoicing and deposits from customers
Accounts Payable	Payments to vendors and purchase orders
Credit cards	Credit Card download and reconciliation processes
Inventory Asset	Synchronization feature
Retained Earnings	Income and expense accounts close every year in this account
Undeposited Funds	Temporary holding place for deposits

Account Structure Using Classes and Jobs or Projects

The Class designation allows you to track account activity and account balances by department, business office or location, separate properties you own, profit centers, or some other meaningful breakdown of your business. Let's say you are a residential home builder and you build single family homes, townhomes, and condominiums. If you set up three classes with these names, QB allows you to use the basic COA for each type of home by tagging transactions with a Class designation. When you run reports, you will see your business activity in three columns with a total column summing up all of the home types.

Now, let's say you have three types of homes within the single family class: Low Income, Median Price, and Luxury. The Job or Project designation allows you to pull reports by type of project within the class single family. So—you can see net profit by type of home (Single Family) and then by type of single family home. You can also track results by type of customer: Retired, Single Professionals, Married Professionals, and Blue Collar Workers, for instance.

These are powerful features that allow you to more effectively manage your business results and avoid setting up multiple accounts in the COA. Take a few minutes now, and think about how you might use these features to track meaningful information regarding your business.

Step 3—Understanding How Accounts Create Reports

QB has a lot of financial reports available to manage your business, but the two reports most often used by financial professionals like bankers, investors, and accountants are the Balance Sheet and Profit and Loss Report, sometimes called an Income Statement. The Balance Sheet is used to help assess the value of a business, while the Profit and Loss Statement (P & L) is used to assess business performance. The Balance Sheet is segregated into three categories and four sub-categories. The P&L Statement has five categories. Each of these categories and sub-categories are populated by QB with data using Account Types and the accounts associated with those types that have been set up in the COA.

The report tables presented on the next pages demonstrate how the QB Account Types translate into report categories and sub-categories. For simplicity, Accounts have not been presented. The Type "Bank" for instance, might have three accounts attached to it, which can be displayed in a detail version of this report.

A few Helpful Definitions:

Current
An asset or liability with a life less than one year is classified as Current. These items are considered liquid—easily convertible to cash without affecting the company's market price. Current Assets divided by Current Liabilities is a common measure of liquidity in the business world.

Long-term
An asset or liability with a life greater than one year is classified as Long-Term. Many Long-Term Assets are assigned a useful life and the cost of the Asset is amortized or depreciated over that life. Long-term Assets and liabilities are used in various ratios to assess a company's solvency. Solvency is a measure of a company's ability to continue as a going concern.

The Balance Sheet

An Assessment of Value

The Balance Sheet presents a snapshot at a single point in time of the net worth of a business or its Equity. Net Worth is calculated using the formula: Assets - Liabilities. In the example below, Assets of $2,100 minus Liabilities of $1,300 = Equity of $800. It is a preliminary assessment of value based on historical cost—the original monetary value of assets and liabilities.

Category	*Sub-Category*	*QB COA Types*		*Amount*
Assets	Current	Bank		100
		Accounts Receivable		200
		Other Current Assets		300
			Total Current Assets	600
	Long-term	Fixed Assets		1,500
			Total Assets	2,100
Liabilities	Current	Accounts Payable		50
		Credit Card		150
		Other Current Liabilities		100
			Total Current Liabilities	300
	Long-term	Long-Term Liabilities		1,000
			Total Liabilities	1,300
Equity		Equity	*Total Equity*	800

The Profit and Loss Statement

An Assessment of Business Performance

The Profit and Loss Statement presents a company's economic performance, referred to as Net Income over a period of time, usually one year. Net Income is calculated by subtracting expenses from total income or revenue. Gross Profit and Net Operating Income are performance benchmarks presented in absolute dollars and as a percentage of total income.

Categories	QB Types		Amount	% Inc
Income	Income		10,000	100%
Cost of Goods Sold	Cost of Goods Sold		5,000	
		Gross Profit	5,000	50%
Expenses	Expenses		3,500	
		Net Operating Income	1,500	15%
Other Income	Other Income		100	
Other Expenses	Other Expenses		(50)	
		Net Income	1,550	16%

As you can see, it is very important to set up the COA properly and associate or tag transactions with proper accounts and account types. It's not that hard once you understand the basic mechanics. It's a bit like putting together a jigsaw puzzle. The Account Types and accounts in the COA are the puzzle pieces. Your job is to properly fit these pieces into two pictures: a Balance Sheet and a P&L Statement. Over time, you will learn what these pictures tell you about the value of your business and its financial performance, and importantly, you will have the information you need for bankers and investors if you find yourself needing some capital.

Learning Topics:

Web Based Features: (Main Ledger Systems)

- Electronic payments and direct deposits
- Payroll processing
- Online bank and credit card processing

Interface Capabilities (Subledger Systems):

- Point of Sales Systems
- Inventory Systems
- Fixed Asset Tracking Programs

Part 3- Interfaces With External Systems

QB is a system that provides the accounting framework for a company via a main transaction ledger (Main Ledger) designed to cost effectively work with business service providers and multifaceted business applications. It contains many web based features and interface capabilities, which help streamline daily operating activities by eliminating time consuming data entry and providing meaningful financial reports. Web based features include electronic payment and direct deposit functions, payroll processing, and online bank and credit card processing.

Interface capabilities include compatibility with numerous Point Of Sales (POS) systems, inventory systems, fixed asset tracking programs[1] and more. Some of these systems are considered independent subledgers that further optimize business operations by allowing a company to track specific types of transactions in a detailed manner with reporting capability not available in QB. Many of these systems allow you to integrate automatically with QB, which on the surface is very appealing, but can reek havoc in your QB Main Ledger system (more on this later).

Right now, I would like you to study the System Overview Chart on the following pages so you can see how all of these systems work together.

---

[1] A fixed asset ledger tracks the purchases and sales of major equipment, furniture, and fixtures. Fixed assets have a life of more than one year. Thus, they are expensed over time and appear on the Balance Sheet during this expensing process.

How All the Systems Work Together

Quick Books is a financial recordkeeping system that allows you to perform Finance Keeping functions using the accounting framework we have been talking about called the Chart of Accounts. Many small companies use QB for all of their bookkeeping and accounting functions. Some small companies in specialized industries and some larger companies use QB in conjunction with independent subledger applications for functions such as payroll, sales tracking, and inventory. Data in these subledgers must be entered into the QB Main Ledger either automatically via a synchronization interface or manually via a periodic Journal Entry at least monthly using a summary report from the subledger system.

Most companies, large and small, are automatically downloading bank and credit card information to eliminate manual data entry of cash receipts and disbursements, and purchases of goods and services. They use the "rules" utility in QB to memorize transaction tagging or coding. Almost all of these companies are using the accounts payable and accounts receivable utilities offered in most QB plans. And finally, some companies are using Class and Project tracking offered in most QB Plans in connection with the COA.

All companies are using some or all of the financial reports available in the QB Main Ledger.

Now—let's take a closer look at how some of these features work together with the QB Main Ledger.

System Overview

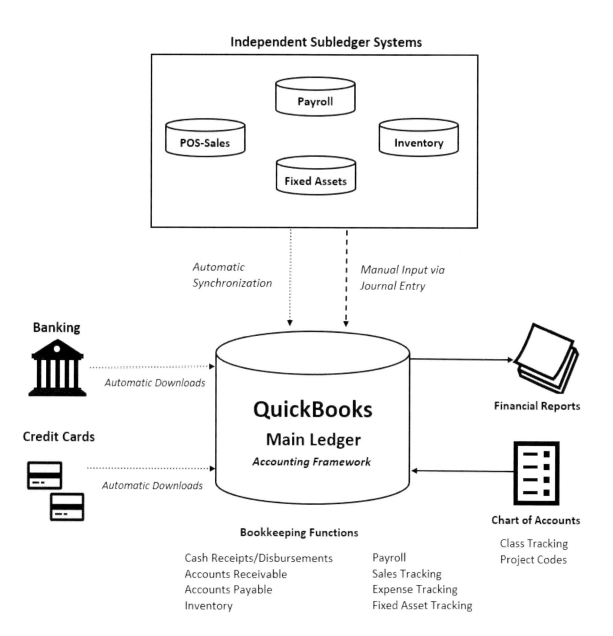

Independent Subledger Systems

POS-Sales · Payroll · Fixed Assets · Inventory

Automatic Synchronization — *Manual Input via Journal Entry*

Banking
Automatic Downloads

Credit Cards
Automatic Downloads

QuickBooks
Main Ledger
Accounting Framework

Financial Reports

Chart of Accounts
Class Tracking
Project Codes

Bookkeeping Functions

Cash Receipts/Disbursements
Accounts Receivable
Accounts Payable
Inventory

Payroll
Sales Tracking
Expense Tracking
Fixed Asset Tracking

Banking, Credit Card, and Payroll Applications

Web based QB features such as online banking and credit card processing automatically populate QB accounts with transactions. Most payroll applications will also automatically populate QB accounts. You simply set up a download link to the proper account in the COA and you're ready to go. For banking and payroll, it will be a bank account of some kind. For credit cards, it will be a designated credit card account. And for all of these accounts, you are expected to do a reconciliation monthly when statements are received. It's simple for the most part, and you do it inside of the QB Main Ledger. That said, here are some "Gotchas".

Banking and Credit Card Transactions

Every transaction that comes down automatically into QB records an entry into a bank account if it's a bank transaction or into a credit card account if it's a credit card transaction. This part is simple. It happens as soon as you allow QB to download from the bank or credit card company. In some QB plans, this happens on its own via the software, but in some QB plans you must click a button or two to initiate the process. The "Gotcha" is that every transaction must have at least two accounts: the credit card or bank account side, which happens automatically, and at least one other account which you must enter for each transaction. Let's examine a simple transaction that might occur in either a bank or credit card download: you purchase some office supplies for $100.00.

In the first case, you pay cash, so there is a $100.00 automatic decrease in your bank account. In the second case, you use your VISA card, so there is an automatic increase of $100.00 in your credit card account. In both cases, you must tell QB to put $100.00 in the Office Supplies account. Below are the QB entries that occur behind the scenes. Italics indicates whether this data is entered manually or automatically by QB.

Purchase of Office Supplies:

		Type	Account Name	Amount		
Case 1	Cash	Asset	Bank-ANB	100.00	Decrease	*Automatic*
		Expense	Office Supplies	100.00	Increase	*Enter*
Case 2	Credit	Liability	Credit Card-VISA	100.00	Increase	*Automatic*
		Expense	Office Supplies	100.00	Increase	*Enter*

Now, let's assume you purchased $50.00 of Office Supplies and $50.00 of Kitchen Supplies. This time you will need to split the transaction into two parts. The entries presented above will look like this.

Purchase of Office and Kitchen Supplies:

		Type	Account Name	Amount		
Case 1	Cash	Bank	ANB Checking	100.00	Decrease	*Automatic*
		Expense	Office Supplies	50.00	Increase	*Enter*
		Expense	Kitchen Supplies	50.00	Increase	*Enter*
Case 2	Credit	Liability	Credit Card-VISA	100.00	Increase	*Automatic*
		Expense	Office Supplies	50.00	Increase	*Enter*
		Expense	Kithen Supplies	50.00	Increase	*Enter*

Once you enter this data for a particular vendor, let's say Office Depot, QB will remember the previous data entry you did. So, the next time a transaction downloads from Office Depot, it will be automatically posted into the accounts previously entered manually. In some QB Plans, you might have to memorize the transaction or set up a rule.

Payroll Transactions

Payroll Transactions behave a little bit differently. Similar to Bank downloads, one side of the accounting entry is automatically loaded into a QB Bank Account, but unlike banking transactions, a payroll transaction usually automatically downloads into two accounts. Thus, if an employee receives a check for $133.28 as presented in the example below, QB will automatically post this amount into a designated bank account and an expense account called Salaries and Wages. Unfortunately, however, the Salary and Wages amount must be adjusted via a manual transaction called a "Journal Entry" because taxes were withheld from the check making the transaction a bit more complicated.

In this example, the employee was actually paid a weekly salary of $150.00, but after the required payroll withholding for taxes, the check was only $133.28. Thus, this transaction must be split into a total of four accounts. You will need to increase the Expense account from $133.28 to $150.00 and then enter three amounts for the tax items the employee must pay.

Employee Payroll Check Entry:

Type	Account Name	Amount		Tax WH
Expense	Salaries and Wages	150.00	Increase	
Expense	Social Security-Employee	(9.30)	Decrease	6.20%
Expense	Medicare-Employee	(2.18)	Decrease	1.45%
Expense	State Tax-Employee	(5.25)	Decrease	3.50%
	Total Employee Taxes	(16.73)		
Bank	ANB Payroll	133.28	Decrease	*Net Check to Employee*

The payroll service provider will usually pay the tax items for you, and when they do, another two-sided transaction will appear on your books: a charge to your bank account and usually a charge to "Payroll Tax Expense". When this happens, they will also pay the Employer share of tax expense including federal and state unemployment taxes, in this case, a total of $39.99. The Employee share of taxes will washout of the account due to the decreases entered in the transaction above. But—if you want to track the various types of Employer Tax Expense in separate accounts as indicated below, a Journal Entry must be made.

Employee Payroll Check Taxes:

Expense	Social Security-Employee	9.30	Increase	Employee Tax Withheld	
Expense	Medicare-Employee	2.18	Increase	Employee Tax Withheld	
Expense	State Tax-Employee	5.25	Increase	Employee Tax Withheld	
Expense	Federal Unemployment-Employer	9.00	Increase	6.00% 1st $7,000 of Salary	
Expense	Colorado Unemployment-Employer	2.79	Increase	1.86%	
Expense	Medicare-Employer	2.18	Increase	1.45%	
Expense	Social Security-Employer	9.30	Increase	6.20%	
Bank	ANB Payroll	39.99	Decrease	Employee and Employer Taxes	

Ok---there's no doubt about it, payroll is complicated, and who wants to make manual entries for every payroll check you deliver. It's a whole lot of work. There is, however, an alternative solution.

Let all the payroll transactions come down automatically and then use a payroll report to make a single adjusting entry in QB for all of these checks. You can do this for each pay period or once a month to save some work. Essentially, you will be making entries for the single paycheck information we just reviewed above for the entire payroll, rather than paycheck by paycheck. QB allows you to set up a template for these kinds of transactions, so it becomes routine once you set up a process to track this information properly. The next example presents the summary journal entries you will make assuming you setup Sub Accounts for the various types of tax expense.

Note:

You will find the numbers you need for a periodic summary entry on the last page of the payroll register. This report might be called by another name like payroll detail report or payroll summary, depending on which service provider you use.

Month End Summary Payroll Journal Entries:

	Type	Account Name	Amount	
Entry 1	Expense	Salaries and Wages	16.73	Increase
	Expense	Social Security-Employee	(9.30)	Decrease
	Expense	Medicare-Employee	(2.18)	Decrease
	Expense	State Tax-Employee	(5.25)	Decrease

This entry increases Salaries and Wages by the amount of employee taxes withheld.

	Type	Account Name	Amount	
Entry 2	Expense	Social Security-Employee	9.30	Increase
	Expense	Medicare-Employee	2.18	Increase
	Expense	State Tax-Employee	5.25	Increase
	Expense	Federal Unemployment-Employer	9.00	Increase
	Expense	Colorado Unemployment-Employer	2.79	Increase
	Expense	Medicare-Employer	2.18	Increase
	Expense	Social Security-Employer	9.30	Increase
	Expense	Payroll Tax (Parent)	(39.99)	Decrease

This entry removes the taxes downloaded lump sum in the Parent Account and records them in Sub Accounts.

Note: Some payroll programs use Payroll Tax Liability and Expense Accounts to track taxes.

Phew! We're done now, and yes, there is a bit of a learning curve here. That's why some companies let their tax accountant make an entry once a year. The problem with this approach, however, is that during the year, accurate payroll information is not available for business planning and cashflow projections. So—I highly recommend you take the time to get this part of your Finance Keeping cycle set-up at least on a monthly basis. It may even save you some money at tax time.

Point of Sales and Inventory Systems

While there are many independent subledger systems available that interface with QB, we will focus on POS and Inventory systems as they are the ones most often used by companies. A POS system is a system with hardware and software that collectively allows a business to accept payments from customers and keep track of sales. It can be used in a store, at a service facility, or "on the go" as you are able to load the app on your phone. An Inventory system is a system capable of monitoring and reporting the cost of producing a product or service. It tracks the cost of both materials and labor from the purchase point, through the production process, and then to the end point of sale. These two systems together provide the data needed for a key performance indicator (KPI) called Gross Margin.

Let's pause for a moment now and take a quick look at this KPI, so you can see how sales and cost information work together to help you manage your business.

The Gross Margin is a key performance indicator for every business as it allows a business owner to feel the pulse of his or her business and measure performance using a margin ratio relative to competitors.

Sales	100,000	*POS System*
Cost of Sales	65,000	*Inventory System*
Gross Profit	35,000	
Gross Profit Margin	35%	*Performance Benchmark*

As you can see, the sales component comes from the POS system and the cost component comes from whatever inventory tracking system a company chooses to use.

Now, the problem with subledger systems is that important data like sales and cost are being tracked in independent systems. Thus, your financial information resides in three different places.

For example, let's say a customer at a farmer's market decides to buy a jewelry box you made in your shop using a credit card. The sale is processed in the POS system. The cost was entered into the inventory system when the box was made. The cash for the credit card payment will be in your QB Main Ledger system when you download your bank account information—three different systems. So—how do we get this information all in one place without a mistake?

Generally, there are two ways to do this.

Option 1: Periodic Journal Entries

Option 1 is fairly easy: enter the information manually using the QB Journal Entry function. It simply requires finding a summary report in the software programs being used with the information you need and dropping this information into the correct accounts via a Journal Entry. The entries, one for sales and one for cost, can be set up in a template. Alternatively, you can duplicate an entry used before and change the numbers each time you need to make an entry, usually at least once a month.

Option 2: Automatic Synchronization of Systems

Option 2 is more complex: automatically enter the information using a synchronization utility available in the independent software programs. While on the surface this is often appealing and most POS and Inventory systems say they integrate nicely with QB, it takes a fair amount of expertise to set up and execute this process properly. Data must be mapped into proper QB accounts and automated utility program triggers[1] must be understood to ensure that sales and cost of sales are entered into proper accounts at the appropriate time. Also, it's important to understand what level of detail will be loaded into the QB system and how it will come down.

Some programs load every transaction into QB with multiple detail items for each transaction every time a transaction occurs, even if the cash has not yet been received. Other programs load transactions on a net basis only when the cash has been received. While this helps with your bank reconciliation as cash is not recorded until received, it makes your sales tax reporting challenging as retail taxes are in a Sales Account lump sum with the sale itself.

---

1 A trigger is an event that causes an automated process to occur.

In summary, here are some "Gotchas" to consider.

• Net entries will require further adjustments via a Journal Entry similar to payroll entries. We will review how to record some of these entries in Part 4.

• Triggers for downloads other than cash create outstanding items in bank account reconciliations.

• Large amounts of details in accounts make financial analysis difficult.

• Inventory triggers for cost reporting when a sale occurs may require special attention and can be complicated.

• Physical inventory counts are still required. Most tax accountants require a physical count at least once a year. Many companies do physical counts monthly to ensure financial information used to manage the business is accurate on a regular basis.

Okay…I hope I have scared you a little. While I absolutely love these independent systems, they can be dangerous. Your books can quickly become a mess if synchronization is not done properly. Thus, I highly recommend Option 1: Manual Entry unless you have both accounting and computer technical expertise available to help you set up a synchronized system and maintain it properly.

Diving into the numbers a bit allows you to:

- *Track where your money is going*
- *Get a loan from a bank, and*
- *Raise money from outside investors.*

Bottom line—it's all about cash!!

Part 4- Accounting Pitfalls

While I have diligently tried to stay away from accounting lessons in this start-up guide, there are some basic accounting concepts which require your attention fairly immediately. Understanding these concepts will help you set up a good COA and tag or code your transactions properly. I will try to keep this discussion short and simple because I know that most of you are not accountants and/or maybe you don't like working with numbers. I get it. Your expertise lies somewhere else.

But—if you want to track where your money is going, get a loan from a bank, or raise some money from outside investors, you need to dive into the numbers a bit. A good set of books is all about money. So let's take a few moments to look at some concepts that will help you avoid some new owner pitfalls.

Basic Concepts to Consider

While there are many ways to tackle the chore of keeping a good set of books, most small companies ultimately use QuickBooks and the Accrual Basis of accounting to manage their business finances. Yes, you can use other programs and maybe even a spreadsheet for a while. You can even use personal bank and credit card accounts to track business transactions. And yes, you can use the cash basis of accounting—you simply track money going into the business and money going out. Many entrepreneurs like to start out this way. They think it's easier and maybe cheaper, but at the end of the day, using less than an optimal system for recordkeeping can result in heartache as your business grows.

Let's talk for a moment about these "simple" methods. They are *not* wrong if you avoid commingling business and personal finances. They are just not optimal.

Spreadsheets and How to Use Them

Spreadsheets are wonderful. I use them all the time. They are great for analysis, for forecasts and projections, for reconciliation of certain accounts at month end, and sometimes as an interface mechanism between third party applications such as payroll programs, and POS and inventory systems. But—spreadsheets can be dangerous when you start using them to do your basic recordkeeping. Here are some of the "Gotchas".

- They are not a database, capable of tracking large amounts of data such as inventory purchases and sales.

- They do not easily and efficiently track information by month, by quarter, and by year needed for financial reporting and tax return filings.

- They do not have any built-in checks and balances to ensure data integrity. The user of the spreadsheet must build-in these kinds of checks and balances into the file design.

- There is no automated reporting. The user must design reports. Thus, the user must prepare reports needed by bankers, investors, and tax accountants.

Bottom line—your primary recordkeeping should always be done in a centralized, organized place with a robust database when it comes to finance matters. If you are tempted to keep your basic financial records in a spreadsheet because you think you will save some money and/or that it might be easier, DON'T DO IT!!! Use spreadsheets to augment your financial reporting and analysis. It's a great tool, not a primary Finance Keeping system.

Business vs. Personal Finance Keeping

The commingling of business finances with personal finances is a serious "no-no". Your personal recordkeeping should be done using a system, manual or automated, that is independent of your business system. This means you should not pay business expenses using a personal checking account or credit card. Even if you choose to be a sole proprietor for a while, use separate business accounts and a separate tracking system to pay your bills for your business and collect money from customers. Many small business friendly banks will offer free checking and savings "Business" accounts. If you are unable to get a "Business" credit card, get a new personal card and use it EXCLUSIVELY for business. Put a "Business" label on the card to avoid improper personal use. Once your business has some stable, profitable history, you should be able to get a Business card.

Here are some serious "Gotchas" when it comes to commingling.

- You may taint the legal protection you have as a LLC or S Corp as your business entity no longer appears to be "separate".

- Tax reporting becomes more complicated and sometimes more expensive as business transactions must be separately reported on tax returns.

- Commingling may negatively impact the "value" of your business if you decide to sell, bring in business partners, raise capital, or exit the business via a public offering.

- Managing cashflow and profitability of your business is difficult as you are not able to readily determine if the business is sustainable without personal funding.

Bottom line—DO NOT COMMINGLE FUNDS!!! Think of your business as a standalone entity with a life of its own.

Cash Basis vs. Accrual Basis of Accounting

Cash basis of accounting is actually a very simple concept. The financial accounts and reports contain only cash transactions—items paid or cash received. Accrual basis of accounting allows a company to record income that has not been received and expenses that have not yet been paid. Essentially, transactions are recorded as they occur, not when money is paid or received. Generally, accrual basis reports are more meaningful for management purposes as they reflect both cash transactions and transactions in progress, resulting in a more comprehensive view of your business results. That said, cash basis information is often preferred for the filing of tax returns as sometimes it delays reporting income until the next year.

The good news is that QB allows you to see your financial results using either method of accounting with a click of a button at the top of every report. The bad news is that the QB cash basis reports are not always true cash basis reports. They may include some accrual accounts because of the way the software works. For the most part, the QB so called "Cash Basis" report is really a "Modified Cash Basis" report. There is nothing to worry about, however, because tax accountants know how to deal with this anomaly.

And now, without getting into anymore technical detail, let me give you two good reasons why you should care about this issue:

1) You want to manage your business using the best information available, and

2) You want your books to be accurate when you send them off to your tax accountant.

I recommend that companies always use accrual accounting during the year. This ensures you are using the best information available when analyzing your company's financial results, assuming you have made all the appropriate adjustments for payroll, inventory, and POS systems. It also assumes you have tagged all transactions with proper accounts, have reconciled bank and credit card accounts at least once a month, and you do not have business transactions in spreadsheets or personal accounts that should be recorded in QB.

Tagging or Coding Accounts

Big picture, every transaction that runs through your books must be associated with at least two accounts in order to find a proper home in QB. This is called tagging or coding. We talked about this earlier, so I won't belabor this point. For many transactions, this tagging or coding is intuitive. Rent, for instance, is a monthly expense coded to Rent Expense, and Postage is coded to Postage Expense. But what about owner compensation or a cash infusion from an owner, the purchase of a copy machine, or a loan payment? These common transactions require a bit more knowledge, but once you get how it works, it becomes routine.

Owner Compensation—a Paycheck vs. a Draw/Distribution

Near and dear to every business owner's heart is compensation. When you worked for somebody else it was easy. You took home a paycheck with tax withholdings and never worried about where the money came from to cover your check or whether or not taxes got paid to the government. As a business owner, however, life is different. There are choices to make about how you get paid, and you are the one covering the payroll and making sure the government gets their share. There are three major ways you can pay yourself and each of them has tax considerations. Most business owners do some combination of all of these methods.

1) You can take a draw or distribution out of the business.

  Draws or distributions are easy. You simply take the cash you need out of the business and record it as a charge in an Equity Account called "Owner Draws or Owner Distributions". Some owners like this method because owner compensation does not appear in the company's P&L Statement as an expense, but—it does effectively reduce the value of your business by taking out some of the cash the company owns. Also, the owner must estimate taxes due on these distributions and make quarterly payments to the IRS and appropriate state tax agencies.

2) You can receive a payroll check.

  Payroll checks are a little bit harder. The company must have a payroll system or a payroll service provider able to process checks, tax withholdings, payments to government agencies, and quarterly payroll tax forms. In this case, the owner receives a paycheck with the appropriate tax withholdings, so no quarterly estimates are required, and the payroll check is reported as salary expense in the P&L Statement. There is one other tax consideration here: your business entity must be registered as a C Corp or S Corp in order for an owner to receive a paycheck. There is no need to worry, however, because if your company is a LLC, the company can make an election to file its annual tax return as a S Corp and still retain its status as a LLC. Your tax accountant should be able to help you with this.

3) You can pay yourself rent as a landlord.

Rent is another easy way to pay yourself as an owner if your business is located on property you own. Effectively, you have a rental agreement between your company and you as a landlord. The rent expense appears on the company's P&L Statement. The business receives a tax deduction for the rent, but the owner as landlord must report the rent as income, which may result in estimated tax deposits during the year if rental income exceeds rental expenses.

Bottom line—tracking owner compensation can be a challenge and should be discussed with your tax accountant.

One other thing...I recommend setting up separate payroll expense and distribution accounts for each owner of the business as owner compensation must be reported separately on tax returns, and owner payroll information needs to be reconciled with Form W-2 at the end of the year.

Owner Contributions—a Loan vs. an Equity Infusion

Every time a business owner deposits his or her personal cash into the company, he or she must decide if the money is a loan to the business or an equity infusion in the form of a capital contribution. Loans appear on the Balance Sheet as a liability and payments must be made to the owner with interest. Contributions also appear on the Balance Sheet, but they are considered Equity. There is no interest, and they are not paid back until and unless the business is sold at an amount at least equal to the total equity in the business at the time of sale. Banks and potential investors like to see some owner equity on the Balance Sheet as it demonstrates the owner's commitment to the business. The owner has so called "skin in the game", they usually say. But that said—if you need the money back, then classify your deposit as an Owner Loan.

Capital Expenditures vs. Expenses

Some items you purchase for your business have a useful life greater than one year. These purchases are called capital expenditures and the cost must be spread out over the useful years. Consider a truck, for instance, with a useful life of five years. When the truck is purchased, it is recorded in a Fixed Asset type account, which appears on the Balance Sheet, and an adjustment is made periodically via a Journal Entry to reduce this cost and record depreciation expense in the P&L Report. The entries look like this.

		Type	Account Name	Amount	
(1)	Check	Fixed Asset	Truck	50,000.00	Increase
		Bank	ANB Bank	50,000.00	Decrease

Record purchase of a truck with 5-year useful life.

		Type	Account Name	Amount	
(2)	Journal	Expense	Depreciation Expense	10,000.00	Increase
		Fixed Asset	Accumulated Depreciation	10,000.00	Increase

Record depreciation expense for the truck at year end.

Notice that the asset is being depreciated on a straight-line basis, evenly over the five year period, a method used by companies required to comply with generally accepted accounting principles (GAAP) issued by the Financial Accounting Standards Board (FASB)[1]. This means the truck will remain on the Balance Sheet until the end of its useful life. For tax purposes, however, the truck may be depreciated on an accelerated basis, and thus, it will appear on the Balance Sheet for a shorter period of time. So—the Balance Sheet for tax purposes will be different than the one used to manage the business on a day to day basis.

Ok...I promised not to get too technical, but I want you to understand that there are differences between a tax set of books and a GAAP set of books, and that GAAP books are required for all public companies and often required by bankers and investors. Also, GAAP basis information

1 The FASB is a private standard-setting body whose primary purpose is to establish and improve GAAP within the US in the public's interest.

helps you manage your business more effectively as you are able to see all transactions in progress in reports and benchmark with competitors.

Now, if an item you purchase has a useful life of one year or less or is under a designated dollar amount, the total cost is recorded in an Expense type account for both GAAP and tax purposes. Most companies establish a policy to expense smaller items completely in the year of purchase to avoid the burden of calculating depreciation on items like this. Usually, this policy is approved by the company's tax accountant.

Loan Payments

When a company receives cash in the form of a loan, a loan account should be set up in the COA. This is usually a Long-term Liability account unless the payback is required in less than a year. Then the Loan account is a Current Liability account. In either case, it appears on the Balance Sheet in the Liability section. When you make a payment, usually monthly, the payment should have an interest component. The coding for these two transactions are presented below.

		Type	Account Name	Amount	
(1) Deposit		Bank	Bank-ANB	10,000.00	Increase
		Liability	Loan-ANB Bank	10,000.00	Increase

Record loan received from ANB Bank.

		Type	Account Name	Amount	
(2) Payment		Liability	Loan-ANB Bank	500.00	Decrease
		Expense	Interest Expense	105.16	Increase
		Bank	Bank-ANB	605.16	Decrease

Record monthly payment on ANB Bank loan.

Note that I am intentionally not referring to debits or credits as these terms can be very confusing sometimes. But you do need to understand that Assets, Liabilities, and Equity on the Balance Sheet and Income and Expenses on the P&L Report are almost always positive numbers. So— be suspicious if you see a negative amount in one of these accounts.

Recording Retail Sales Transactions

If you own a retail company or sell parts to customers, you will have to manage the sales tax process in QB, which can be challenging if you report in multiple states, cities, and counties and/or use a POS System. As you probably know, sales tax is generally a pass-through charge on materials sold to customers. This means that the tax collected from the customer is paid to the governing agency without any impact on profit and loss in the business. In some states, there may be a discount offered for paying these taxes on a timely basis and completing the required forms. If this is the case, the discount is reported in a Sales Tax Adjustment account, an Income Type account, in the P&L Report. Let's take a look now at these basic transactions.

Sales Tax Transactions Processed Directly in QuickBooks

Sales transactions with tax implications processed in QB are usually managed using a liability account and an income account. Tax collected from the customer via an invoice or a credit card transaction is recorded as an increase in the liability account, and tax paid to the governing agency is recorded as a reduction in this account. This is a very simple process as what you collect is equal to what you pay absent any discount allowed and a timing difference at month end because you collect the amount from customers during the month and pay the governing agency the following month. The transactions in QB look like this.

	Type		**Account Name**	**Amount**	
(1) Deposit	Bank		Bank ANB	1,100.00	Increase
	Liability		Sales Tax Payable	100.00	Increase
	Income		Laptop Computer	1,000.00	Increase

Record cash collected from customer for a computer sale.

	Type		**Account Name**	**Amount**	
(2) Payment	Liability		Sales Tax Payable	100.00	Decrease
	Income		Sales Tax Adjustment	2.00	Increase
	Bank		Bank ANB	98.00	Decrease

Record tax payment to governing agency.

After the first transaction takes place the balance in the Sales Tax Payable account that appears on the Balance Sheet will be $100.00 at month end, the amount reported on the Sales Tax Return. When the tax is paid the following month in the second transaction, this balance will clear. If you are paying taxes to multiple government agencies by separate check, you might want to set-up a Sub Account for each agency under the Parent Account called Sales Tax Payable.

Sales Tax Transactions Using a POS System

As you know, many businesses use a POS application to process sales transactions. Using a POS sales app often simplifies credit card transactions as the service provider collects the cash from the various credit card companies and remits it to the business owner net of a service fee. They collect cash for the sale itself, for sales taxes (state, city, and county), and then charge a fee for this service. Many service providers send monthly statements so you can reconcile this activity similar to reconciling a bank or credit card account. They also provide comprehensive tax and sales reports which can be used to adjust your QB accounts and file your sales tax returns.

That said, beware, some service providers deliver reports that have all the information you need to record transactions in QB, but are very difficult to use. This is important because sales transactions usually come down *net* into QB, so you have to adjust your accounts via a Journal Entry using provider reports. Let's take a look at a single transaction. In this example, the amount hitting your cash account is $5.19 and the amount hitting your sales income account will probably be the same. You will need a Journal Entry to record the sales tax and the fee, but that's not all.

Deposit Breakdown	Amount		QB Accounts
Sale		$ 5.00	Product Income
Tax	8.6%	0.43	Sales Tax Payable
Collected		5.43	
Fee	4.8%	(0.24)	Service Fee-POS Provider
Cash Received		$ 5.19	*Cash--automatic side of the entry*

Many service providers pay periodically, say every two or three days. Thus, when a deposit is posted to your bank account, it may contain multiple transactions, complicating your bank and service provider reconciliations, especially at month end if the provider statement reflects transactions that don't post to your bank account until the following month. If your provider does send a monthly statement, reconciliation is usually much easier. You can compare your bank statement to the provider statement. But if you don't get a statement, you must find a provider report, maybe more than one, that will help you do this kind of comparison.

In Summary

Retail sales transactions can be challenging. Be sure you understand your reporting requirements and purchase the QB plan that gives you the help you need. If you plan to use a service provider to process your sales, be sure you understand how transactions will download into QB and what reports are available to help you reconcile accounts and make required adjustments. Most importantly, if you get stuck, be sure to get some help immediately. Sometimes, you can educate yourself online, but sometimes you may need to pay for the help of an expert.

Inventory Purchases

Inventory purchases should be recorded in the Inventory account, which is a current asset type of account that appears on the Balance Sheet. When the inventory is sold, it is removed from the inventory account and recorded as Cost of Goods Sold, which appears on the P&L Report. This adjustment is done either via a Journal Entry periodically when assets are sold, or automatically recorded via the company's inventory system. It is a good business practice to adjust your inventory at least once a month for these asset sales. It is also a very good practice to conduct a physical inventory monthly and record any noted obsolescence as an expense at month end.

Undeposited Funds

The Undeposited Funds Account is a place to store customer payments until you deposit them in your bank account. Once you have your deposit slip, you can combine these payments into a single record so that transactions in your QB cash account match transactions posted in your bank account. For instance, you enter five checks in QB, then run to the bank and make one deposit for all five checks. When you get back to the office, you can combine the five QB checks into one transaction so that your bank statement matches the items posted in your QB cash register. It sounds like a wonderful feature, but—this is a Utility Account and it must be managed properly. Duplicate entries for deposits and income may occur if left unattended, and these entries are hard to correct. So, if you're going to use this feature, be sure you understand how it works or just turn it off. You don't need it to manage your cash.

Ask My Accountant Account

The Ask My Accountant Account is a place to store transactions when you don't know how to tag or code them. It is supposed to be a temporary holding account for Finance Keepers who need to get help from a professional regarding the proper way to record a transaction. The problem is that it can become a dumping ground if left unattended, and the longer it sits, the larger it usually gets, and the harder it is to clean it up.

So—I recommend that you avoid this account, maybe even delete it, so you aren't tempted to use it on a regular basis. Get the help you need right away to record transactions properly. If you can't find the answer you need on the internet, then call an accountant as soon as possible.

Monthly Closings

The business world generally runs on monthly cycles. You will receive bank, credit card, and loan statements monthly. Vendors like utility companies, landlords, and internet service providers send monthly bills. Customers usually pay their bills on a monthly basis, and many government agencies require monthly compliance reports. Thus, Finance Keepers are expected to do what is called a "Monthly Close", which generally means that all significant accounts are analyzed and reconciled on a monthly basis, and financial reports are reviewed within at least 10 business days after month end.

I recommend using a monthly checklist based on your company's COA to complete this process. You simply list all the accounts to be reviewed in a column. Then going across the page you have a column for each month of the year. At the end of each month, after you complete your work for each account on the list, you put a check mark or date in the box indicating you have completed the work. It's as simple as that, and it helps you stay in touch with your business.

A Quick Final Review

And now, before we part ways and you get started getting your books up and running, let's review the overall process proposed in this guide. Remember, the goal is for you to have a stable accounting system ready to manage your finances by the time you are ready to start making money.

- **Select the right finance system.**

  Using the template provided, assess what your finance system requirements will be for the next two years. Then select the QB Program you want, Online vs. Desktop, using the Program Comparison Chart. And finally, choose a QB plan using the Plan comparison charts.

- **Set-up your chart of accounts.**

  Once you have chosen a QB Plan, it's time to set up your COA. But before you get started, be sure you understand how Accounts are structured, what role utility accounts play, and how Accounts create financial reports.

- **Set-up the interfaces you want with external systems.**

  Most companies use the QB web based features for online banking, credit card processing, and payroll. These download links should be set-up as part of your COA work. If you have decided to use a POS, inventory, or other external system, set-up what you need to properly integrate these system(s) with QB.

- **Avoid common accounting pitfalls.**

  Before you begin tagging or coding accounts, make sure you understand how to record contributions, owner compensation, loan payments, sales tax, inventory, and capital expenditures. Importantly, do not commingle personal and business transactions.

About The Author

I was born in Chicago, Illinois and now live with my husband, Steve, on the western slope of the Rocky Mountains in Colorado. I am an author and the founder of Butterflies Pause Inc., a nonprofit organization promoting healthy mental awareness through imagery and the written word. I have authored a series of healing books, a soul anthology, a memoir, and various instructional material for business entrepreneurs.

I am a CPA with a master's degree in Finance and a certified volunteer business consultant with the Colorado Small Business Development Center (SBDC) funded by the U.S. Small Business Administration (SBA). Prior to my retirement, I owned my own business for 10 years and worked for various entrepreneurs in the start-up and development mode for 30+ years.

My work can be found online at the website presented below.

You may contact me at debbie@butterfliespause.org or visit me online at www.butterfliespause.org.

Made in United States
North Haven, CT
28 March 2023

34674837R00033